Teethmarks

Teeth

marks

Sina Queyras

Nightwood Editions
Roberts Creek, BC

Published by
Nightwood Editions
RR#22, 3392 Beach Avenue
Roberts Creek, British Columbia V0N 2W0
www.nightwoodeditions.com

Edited by Triny Finlay
Typesetting by Silas White
Printed and bound in Canada

THE CANADA COUNCIL | LE CONSEIL DES ARTS
FOR THE ARTS | DU CANADA
SINCE 1957 | DEPUIS 1957

BRITISH
COLUMBIA
ARTS COUNCIL
Supported by the Province of British Columbia

Nightwood Editions acknowledges financial support from the Government of Canada through the Canada Council for the Arts; and from the Province of British Columbia through the British Columbia Arts Council.

Library and Archives Canada Cataloguing in Publication

Queyras, Sina
        Teethmarks / Sina Queyras.

Poems.
ISBN 0-88971-193-3

        I. Title.

PS8583.U3414T43 2004   C811´.6   C2004-904491-5

This book is for my parents.

TABLE OF CONTENTS

Jersey Fragments

Dizzy, or, My Mother's Life as Cindy Sherman

Eight Small Stones

Bridging & Tunnelling

Jersey Fragments

THREE SONGS FOR JERSEY

1.

Welcome to the hourglass. Doormat or
escape hatch, depending on what side
of the Hudson you call home. Verdant
once was state of industry and strip clubs,
nail shops and roadways, soprano land cum back door
of America. Birthplace of Ginsberg and Williams. Slim
remembrance of Whitman in ginkgo leaves and crumpled
Budweisers; in rusted pumps along Route 1 all the way to Camden;
in the three-legged dog who wanders up the turnpike; the rain
silky and thick as liquid detergent; the egret who poses
by the sunken tires, or the turtles who sun on rubber-filled ponds.
Welcome to the state of hearts: the black man
at the New Brunswick station who tips his hat, the beautiful,
thick-jawed, high-haired women who stand waiting at the train;
the wide-hipped, smart-mouthed waitresses of the Bagel Dish,
the saucy women waiting on Route 27 for the Atlantic City bus.
I can give you the insides of books, take you through the shelves
of the New York Public Library or I can take you to the train,
smelling enchiladas and Starbucks, oh I am composing this
while walking, listening to Lucinda Williams in the rain.

2.

Not the last train to Philly, or New York, nor the last Amtrak,
and the buzz of trucks on Route 18, and Route 1, and the turnpike,
and the Garden State, and the 287, goes all night. I remember sleeping
on the highway outside Prince Rupert at fifteen, miles from Alaska
and not a car from 2 till 6 when the first logging truck rumbled by, how
we never saw animals close to the road then and I wish
we did not now. I imagine fitting tiny cotton puffs for the birds,
knitting earmuffs for the deer, worry that suddenly they will snap,
stand on two legs, take advantage of the Gun and Tackle's excellent
layaway plan, hoof themselves on the turnpike and shoot out tires,
one and one and one.

3.

All winter I come searching for song: stalk the smoky armlet
scraping between the pulsing power lines and demonstration garden,
to the painted tidal river with its oil drums and plastic,
with its uncountable chemicals. I bristle the common teasel,
hard-nosed matron of multifarious grasses: spike, timothy,
quack and rye, which I part with my giant eye unearthing
horsebalm calyx with its panicled branches; the rattling
tripartite pods of the wild lily. Worthless field, figworts lance
as I zoom in on the toothy jimson weed, its jawed membrane,
prodigious artillery. Here and here, vines twist around sycamore.
I step on broken glass and mallow, climb over chunks of concrete
and coffee cups where last year a killdeer baited me from her nest.
Under the steady bass line of Route 1, I find water bottles and condoms;
echoes of the white-throated sparrow, and the summer fair.
But the only song these days is the grackle—that franchisee
of the bird world: metallic, black: shook foil in the pharmaceutical air.

AFTER HE'S GONE

Every word you held back hangs
like pollen. And what you thought
of giving, but did not, bumps

a rosary of intention. Unknown
paths abundant as dime-store
gems, and after dinner

you lie on the sofa slipping
your hand down your jeans,
suddenly clear that this was all

that could be done after pork chops
and six hungry mouths. Later,
you find yourself smoking cigars,

drinking port in a perpetual toast.
And when your mind narrows, and
your heart clings, you remember

how his chest felt when you tucked
that final note in his jacket pocket,
and you feel your spine lengthen.

YOU TURN MY HEAD

Blue jays pry the dawn.
Your blue eyes:
yesterday's worry melting.

Sappho I dream your thumbs
firm as fragments on my thighs.

Now the starlings pull
a tangled veil across the sky.

Amma pirouettes.
Even here the tea
is always cold.

In Jersey, cicadas
taunt pumpkins:
we are all avoiding.

STRUCK MATCHES

This morning your breasts
are statuary, brow of a woman
who could stand in a harbour for a hundred years.

On aubergine linen we lounge, full
prow and longing for something hard
and easy: palm on palm we

are dreaming each other in leather,
we are dreaming each other
licking our way to France.

You reach for your glasses, I roll and
press on, the morning news already
imprinted on my mind: how

many will die today so that we
can be hot and bored; lives spread
so thin we have forgotten what we are.

DRIVING TO BROOKLYN, SPRING

Wrong turn on Staten Island: not
the first, but today a pocket full
of pistachio shells, mind full

of Winnipeg: "Noter Dame," swells
of snow; tobogganing in pairs on the pursed
banks of the Red River; the fluorescent

green, orange and yellow shoes of
my first day of school, so far
from Riverview Elementary now. Still,

fool I am mourning Mrs. Anderson's
ankles. A penis shy under willows; hitting
Ritchie (who by Christmas would have lit

his toybox on fire) over the head
with a plastic pot because even then
I could not even pretend to cook for a boy.

THE DEER OF NEW JERSEY

Somerset. Colts Neck. Teaneck. Last exit to The Land of Make Believe. What is Columbus Day and who celebrates it? Which exit? What miracle of independence. Parcel and parcel the land. What is Stacked Plates Rock? How can we capitalize? Lulav. Etrog. Rosh Hashanah over now. Halloween on the heels. Pagan, Jew, Arab. Deer trails. Gas stations. Concrete tripping. Garbage bags line Route 206 past horse farms. What is faith? What is economy? Who are the Vikings now? Pharmacy and pharmacist. Welcome to the chemical century. Welcome to the genetic world. Blue sky. Air and water. Tree and vine, tree and vine. Onward to the Delaware Water Gap. How can we tap that? Lush and cut stone. Where is Amiri? What general crossed here? Moon vibes. Roadkill. Pumpkins for sale. *Kill Osama* bumper stickers. What is long gone? What is democracy? Was there ever a centre? What held? For how long? Where is your Benjamin Franklin? Deer trails. Highways. Long ago moccasins. Muffled in the woods. Flags trampoline the air. Mouths wide open. Whose? What is bouncing? Thighs hot on the seat—yours. Nine hawks at the cloverleaf circling. Who is hunting whom? Flag draped over the Arabian Stallion. What is patriotism? Burnt sumac. Squirrel food. Heading off to Afghanistan. Deer with bent necks. Bloodied mouths. What is terror? Delicate lips. Someone says they are hoping for domestication. Tender hooves. Bean irritant. Hoof on track. SUVs and delivery vans. This car heading north. Why don't deer migrate north? Where do terrorists migrate? Where is away from this? Roadside eyes. Encounters with nature. Everything burning. Cars inflamed. Radar and radar, maple and oak. Sunoco and McDonald's. Oil fields, oil spills. Shell is us. Gulf is you. Chevrons point the way in.

ASHES

She is crouched on a slope of ash as I shovel.
Scatter me, she says, not only in the mountains,
but at the cinema, on the Seawall. Her hands

hang, heavily oiled wings. Hovel me, she
says, on the soccer field near Chinatown,
on Granville Island, off the ferry to Mayne,

on the Sunshine Coast, carry me to the vein
of an arbutus, in salal and moss lay me down.
Unaware she is, of our father furtive, a brown

paper bag in hand. Only when I call
does she look up: both of them blank,
barricaded. What does he carry? Now

I remember he is already gone, frown
that she is going. But aren't we all?
Why put the landing before the fall?

WHAT BOOKS OUR LIVES HAVE BECOME

You pajamaed. You with hair frizzed,
you with your eighteenth-century head.
You with Rochester tonguing

lurid suggestions, Swift holding
court in our bedroom, applause
so loud that some nights it is

I who pull out the paddle
and spin the tub (yes, I know
there was no tub). But

this tale is too cerebral. We
have forgotten the chafe of skin.
Devout, I dream Woolf, wafer-

thin under our bed, hungry,
hungry and yet, she'll eat not
a page if this is the stuff. Now

she pecks messages on the wall:
the world is a woman, a tower
with expandable hard drive:

try violet (not violent) ink;
upgrade often, back up files.
Never repent.

ME VICTORIOUS

Me with my new blue jeans and t-shirt from the Gap; me with pink underwear and a goldfish shower curtain from Target; me with my full tank of gas and my recycling stacked. Me victorious in red, white and blue, in clean socks and discount hair; me victorious and tummy full. Me about unconditional market rules. Me about not caring whether our socks are made by infants in Bangladesh, our potatoes sprayed on the outside, or encoded with pesticides in their genes, because who has time to worry about that? Who cares if companies can own our DNA just as long as we don't have to read that fine print, and hey, if they're encoding pesticides in DNA, why not antibiotics in us? Why not Valium or Prozac? And while they're at it, why not do away with the gene that makes some of us gay, funny, serene, artsy, bohemian, overly or underly enthusiastic, doubters, promoters, bad joke-tellers, union sympathizers, shamans, men who clean. Whatever makes some of us lean the opposite way—whatever opposite is this week. Just as long as I don't have to think about potatoes in soil: I prefer to think of french fries all golden and salted, so far removed from the earth that I believe they are a lab invention, shot out of a potato gun at one hundred fries per second. I mean I'm okay with that. I'm okay with unidentifiable transactions, the elimination of wild unless it's between the sheets and involving me, oh, me oh me victorious. Me about owning stuff. Me about buying power and income security. Me victorious over slippages, over fractures of wonder, over instances of compassion. Me only concerned with interest rates, credit card limits, cheap flights to hot places where the sun oh, oh sun, oh sun shines twenty-four-seven and water is chlorinated, contained in cement and plastic, trucked in from places where other people have to endure rain. Me victorious. Me such a fine citizen, such a good statistic, such a humble consumer, I vote with my fashion sense, with my belly, with my God—and he's mine, all mine only listens to me—turns his back on you, all you, other types. Me, oh, me victorious with my credit card, with my well-heeled acceptance, with my condoning and tolerance, my blind eyes, my skill at skirting you on the street, my ability to step over, to go around, to sink lower, my cavernous depths of denial. Me victorious over sleepless nights. Over worrying. Me Nyquil, me Sleep Ease, me Johnny Walker, me Budweiser, me Imitrix, me a totally hot babe. Me laser aerobics, me a new Volkswagen Golf, me Googling, me Googled, me full of the best intentions, me a suicide bomber with a long, slow burn, me just want the Dream, me want the lottery, me want that chance, me just want to believe the only thing holding anyone back is their own lack of hard work.

WAITING FOR OWL

Tonight you walk out with your tea, heel
of bread, tomato sauce dripping
on your Cat in the Hat slippers.
You wish you'd worn a sweater now, only
a few steps back to the cabin but dusk
is so brief and you've heard the owl's wing
silent. You stand in the path, hesitate, turn
to leave but your feet stick firmly. You twist,
crack your spine, roll your shoulders,
settle into your vigil—it may be tonight
wingspan fills the path, blocks the sun's
crimson descent. This is how life goes: never
knowing whether owl will show, wondering
if you're on the right path, naked
as the other animals of the world crack peanuts,
elbow each other, point at your kneecaps, elbows,
silly thumbs, mouth open and useless, unable
to call owl, or sing up the moon.

THE BLESSING

1.

After several desperate freeway phone calls,
the priest glides his Honda into my father's parking spot.
Honda. Father. He is a younger man, and Russian,
my mother tells me. Come to bless the house,
my father's birthday, the first since his death.
But before the blessing, she wants the crucifix hung
—my father had taken it down, she explains,
to clean the walls for her weeks before collapsing
on the bathroom floor. Standing on the bed now
in his socks, the priest confesses
that he is not cut out for such tasks,
and I imagine all over the world, nuns
on stepladders.

2.

When the priest asks for a glass of water,
she brings him filtered. And when he dips
his fingers in, raising his pudgy hand
to the same crucifix I kissed the nailed
feet of as a child, her bark
knocks him off the bed. Now
he holds an ice pack, attempting
to convince that any water he touches
is holy. But she'll take no chances. She pulls
down the bottle from Lourdes; the same water
I had splashed on my forehead those nights
I was ill. *You think it's still good?* he asks,
and she says, *There's no due date on holy water
my boy*, praying this is true.

Dizzy, or,
My Mother's Life as Cindy Sherman

Men act and women appear. Men look at women.
Women watch themselves being looked at.

–John Berger, *Ways of Seeing*

]running away
]bitten

–Sappho, trans. Anne Carson, Fragment #58

UNTITLED FILM STILL #35

Oh,
her hips,
   babies hang. For men
      a doorway
   arm
rift of
   flesh and
they move through her
   daily. She offers
bread, soup, lure
of open beaks.

Of course
   setting up house
      on an angle
   having babies
filling space, everything new
   one thing
maintaining another.

Where is the emotional budget
for stasis?

She polishes the floor
tugging
   babies

UNTITLED FILM STILL #11

Nothing about her says
notice
pins in her hair
and
sleeps on her side.

These shoes weren't
for cleaning, but
                    bleach
   shag
        long is tedious, short
        brown
   colour   headache.

Her husband's men paw
the air.

This is not the Bates
        still eyes in the plastic
framed, oh
        and peach tiled
tidy enough for wrists

Come at noon you'll see her sprawled
        it is not what she wants,
(yes it is) no, it is
what she knows.

TV M/OTHER

She watches her m/
other
self   round in a
black and white
Remember
            channels?

            Correction,
she does not watch
herself,
            turns
(Look it's on!)
            when she
is on: aproned
smiling, grocery list
mind.

The gaps are not:
            visible
(of course)   or squint.
It could be comical.
When the camera
pans to his stubble
and pec

      the women
              wall to wall

vacuum,

feather duster
      rabbit
tail. You never see
her (after mid-
night)

fingers, lips, hair
loosening, frayed
at the end,

or longing.

      Dead babies
line the cellar
stairs

Come.

(oh come, come on)

SONG FOR THE OPEN ROAD #1

Give a woman a car, don't
expect her home for ham
and happenstance.
You think Beaver's mom?
Did you see Lucille?
She is a woman who knows
          but where

CAR INTERIOR #1

Imagine speeding   spit
rail of highway
lonely, night: no lights,
      roadside bar
            rock and tree.

Even here that look
can knock a semi off the road.

Even here
truckstops edge closer
when she
passes.

LATE NIGHT MOVIES

She finds daytime
Valium. For mothers it is
            indoors: white
walls, white
            white

Even the beautiful ones, she

watches
            Bette
            Joan
            Katherine (shrill)
vinyl and spin, what
            has she paid
for that life?

She is not willing
          loves
strength
          muscle
                    over
what

her cigarette
slays them: eyes too, mouth
blood, even (her life)
black and white

(in between shoes
after midnight
in the chief and globe glow
and
of electrons)

UNTITLED FILM STILL #5

Words
        she doles out daily
sweet limbs

Piñata head, she
moves between desk
file cards
    not
        the kind
served with
        cocktails.

        You want this
to be from a lover,
but it is from a nun, each
spring a knot
sex   blanket
mountains.

Not virgin.
Too red
for that.

Where are her?
Where is his?

(hush
she dreams)
but
it does not
and barbed
her cat's tongue
barbed.

CAR INTERIOR #2

        she runs.   Moose sunset; into
forest of   Lights
rerun
        the prisoner.

She goes alone
        car
        and
smoke of the butt
himself on her thigh.

For all of you who say leave, try
running with a six-pack
        (these ones talking, these ones
with noses runny and even *shush!*)
        demands.
She wants to freeze them
        hold them manageable,
an audience
        not
        talking back.

ROADSIDE MEMORY #1

Five kids and
pee
construction. Cars crawling
        beetles on
sweltering
and muffled
        mops her breasts, tulip
and ochre shift, floral, sweat (her waist,
he can put his hands around her waist).

She points   neon
        a lighthouse, but he will not
never will do what she wants,
needs
        crying
she throws herself out
of the moving Valiant (black
red interior, red beaks) and walks:
it is Calgary. 1959. A man at a desk
lurid, puce (she understands this now) face
pockmarked but still, manners: May I?
        she feels the sweat
in her brassiere, imagines a swimming pool
the sound of slot machines, nickel and dime
(Oh God, the heat)
in the hall. Lack of air

(someone has leaned on the prairie,
elbow of shale, thumb of treeline)
   almost turning back, hoping
     at the side of the road,
       impatience. Angry. Controlling. Door
corrugated small, knob
   and foul. Shaving mirror light bulb, window
(Who brought the f'ing cat? Who lost the house? Who could not
pay the bills?) and someone knocking.

This is private,
her dress. She hovers, trembling
   a lady never sits
(she is faint now) and suddenly banging
in here, she says again, face seeping,
scurry of   in the sink
   here, she says, again, harder, now
   she sways

pees on her shoes, reaching
to the sink for balance, pulls
now scrambles, yelling
pounding. She opens the window
as far as she can and cat-thin
            midsection of
hip bones bruised
she stands on the sink, snaps her
hips, hinges through
dirty laundry, head
first into
clatter of garbage

UNTITLED FILM STILL #65

All her attempts to fade
into landscape fail.

Yes, she wears red:
a response.

Verses knock the miles
                    refrain
          cigarettes
          lit
extinguished,
She
slices
          night sky
          her eye
                    (already lined)
          her eyes cut a path
          all the way
to

WHY SHE STAYS

He undoes her
       continental drift
             honeybees and
      memory
of stinkweed.
Mystery of geography
of lines twice followed.
Scent of
      or
wondrous
      and
disarmed.

SONATA BETWEEN 1 AND 3

1.

Everywhere surfaces (rub
      don't rub)
She does not
       for

is a

2.

No one has calves
like hers, a runway
shimmy
She wishes
she had known how
lovely is to marry

Nothing for its own sake
but

3.

School
is a blessing
she wakes
after noons (ah)

4.

    stretches
before her a
full packet
    tear the foil
and
a meditation, the shape

of
    passing.

5.

Some days
      Susan Hayward
      on death row
nothing
but
and nothing
  change into.

6.

No, it isn't
      really.
It's
      and promises,
and what if
the only way
is not to
      Where
would
go?

7.

She dips
          cool of memory
a lake.

woman
          haystack,
woman
          lips.

          other
lips
          harsh
in the truck
passing
or
back from
      having passed her
by.

THE STALKER

He snaps
      babies on the bed, bathed
smelling like   all teeth
and hair.

     her on
     sofa,
lounging—as if this
is what she does
all day—ashtray
balanced between
     breasts.

them
     baptism

   her
     bowling trophy
        Eiffel Tower
legs

THE ROUND-UP CAFÉ

Even a motel diva
gets hungry.
Who
        deliciously tragic
        relish
behind those glasses, under
that coat anyone
but a blonde
might disappear

coffee, thin veil
        and trench
(tell me I'm a good

GOOD WOMAN MOMENT

       all day
and potato salad   spring
       rubber tires
emaciated fox
       cigarette butts
and watermelon

If she could
       (can anyone see me?)
       hold this moment

he
and straps a pot roast
on the radiator

drives in circles
       little legs and feet
mountains and
cooked through.

Later in the clean sheets
       throughout the house

buds everywhere at once.

UNTITLED FILM STILL #50

Everything rubbed
     past   burned
beyond
        purge of the
eager
     to let go and acquire.

nation of shape-shifters
     minds. White walls, tapered
legs, blonde
     shiny, everything
easy to clean, everything
easy. Lean, she weighed in
at ninety-seven pounds before
     after
babies. Cold, is her mantra
     huddled
a cigarette. Silence. Lonely. You
cannot imagine how much space
between thoughts.

WAYS OF SEEING

Tissue and lace gown, orderly, maudlin,
letter, crumpled chenille, photo, candle burning, hairspray
long blonde hair, huge ass, tits, uncased pillows spearmint
leaves, sugar-coated, Wrigley's white, romance novel, black
silk, bare legs, mouth slightly always slightly open,
in black bra, lace panties, silk robe, floral sheets holding
a mirror flat, arm crooked,
on knees, with suitcase, leaving,
no flowers,
in wool suit, parting the curtains, offstage or
purse open, no more Valium, martini glass, black glasses, with
hats, as gestures, frantic, lost, scoopable
as doorstops and lightning rods, high and busty
as heart-shaped openings, as slots
runways, plots, points of entry, nightstands
to hold keys and open bottle tops, as lemons and pears
tripods and backdrops, vacuum cleaner handles, scrubbing
toilets, suction cups, eating caviar with men on their arms

in furs, with bank accounts,
carrying grocery bags, waiting in motel rooms,
sneaking out nights:
those who face tall buildings,
who open doors,
who open letters,
who plumb,
who swim,
who know what their tits are up to, huddled
in caves, waiting.

SNAPSHOT OF MY MOTHER IN NATURE

In case you didn't know
Nature
is dirty:
no hamburgers
hard to walk
in heels.

ROADSIDE MEMORY #2

Of course he is not
She yells   cars!   Workmen!
(story of my life) Desperate
red and fuming. Heels
blackbirds   police car. She
at her legs   the roots , black
purseless, no cigarettes
babies. Listen here!
uniformed
raised eyebrows
who?
why would a man run
(she has a run, she does run) he

leave his wife? This

insinuation. Interrogation
motel
she is from
now in her cell
crying. *They must be injured*, she says.

They must be
or

Her husband
        to her. Her good husband
                        children
provider.

black hair   not shaved (she
can't remember stubble)

Valiant. *He is a big man*

and broad

Listen, there were
        screws   putrid
walls, little bathroom

undone.

violent.   no dinner.

Finally she calls her sister   vouches
        (claimed
a voucher exists, key)

        Suddenly coffee
donuts, Caramilk bar, blanket, a policewoman.

She sits   of course she is

And later
the car
        motel   sleeping   children
like ducklings
        like ducklings

duck

UNTITLED FILM STILL #54

She moves only at night   sheer
       air and linen
She is forty-two
       dyed
       turns her collar
turns back a pillar
       of
dips
       the Tropicana
school night but
       she is singing   elegant
runway
of skin

This is allowed   this
is not allowed not done
won't do
dues not paid

Lights
                in a stream.
Polynesian Christmas music. Women
in grass skirts serve her (blissful
escape). She has never had
concoctions
                and fruit
                                loves the umbrella.

her head unfolds.
                shivers, pulses

lights a cigarette. She is
                desert and
flare on the roadside another
near miss. She has, is, contains too much
                is escorted back home
where he is sleeping

UNTITLED FILM STILL #7

1.

the door opens
      and drives south.
      Denny's   Ford
Mall. She
passes the school where her children

She continues: Whalley, White Rock,
Bellingham, glides over the coastal mountains
heat and luck of the south

Midnight and she stops
for a coffee at the Denny's. Trucks

She is free. She is
on the run
home a rumour
pause between

       peaks
now Salem, Eugene, diner
and slope, not stopping
          spectacle of open
landscape and road, wagon
trains and now
Chrysler, green
rooted only
to her. She

(don't stop)

       only for gas
cheeseburger, shake
and by midnight the biggest little
       buzz
her husband's paycheque
       slot machines
       wins nothing, loses nothing. She is
afraid to sleep, afraid she is
not awake.

2.

       packed nothing
she buys glasses, a new dress
new bra for the new
(there, cocktail, cigarette, how
her heel twists at the ankle)
shoes in years.

calves
      and tingles

There is a woman   sunhat
patio
unencumbered
     or anyone. She will not

her skirt up and rubs
           does not flinch
(can anybody see me?)

3.

    Blackjack. She
stands between two tables,
       both at once. Can't find
a good dealer. If she thinks
         crying, beaks
snapping
she will never
return

there is a key
and a lock
it slides into

a well, not a good one
that she sings out of
steps outside
finally outside
         the frame

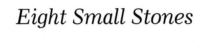

Eight Small Stones

NIGHT FLANNEL

The night is fuzzy with streetlights and the creaking of doors, and the light in her room flashes on and she is scooping her out of bed in her new flannels, pink sheets wrapped tightly and they are into the Valiant and passing by other houses, and streetlights. Outside the brick and neon, people sway, and in the lobby a dwarf stands in a doorway pulling passersby into a room full of smoke and coloured lights and a woman in a fur coat is yelling that she hasn't had too much, in fact she hasn't had enough, may never have enough, and who is he to tell her when she has to stop? There is a cubbyhole in the wall and a man with a cigar and shiny head winks at her and her sheet, elbows leaning on the rows of candy and gum, framed by cigarettes and bags of potato chips and for a moment she thinks she has gone to the fair, the one at Lake Winnipeg in the summer, but there is a scuffle and the woman in the fur flies out the swinging doors and her mother slips into an elevator, pulling her head close to hers so that she can smell smoke and lavender perfume, so that she can hear her heart racing, breath raspy and shallow, and then her cheek brushes hers and is wet. When the doors open the light changes and she licks a tear from her mother's cheek, the way she always licked hers, and her mother moans so deeply it makes them both shake as she turns the key to the little one-bedded room.

NIGHT ROAD

It is midnight when they pull away from the house, her collection of 45s, The Bay City Rollers, Jackson Five, stacked in the unfinished basement. Her father's truck is loaded with grease guns and tool chests, smelling of wine-tipped cigarillos and coffee. Snow slices sideways in the headlights. She has told him about each of her classes, how she dreamed of flying, and now he puffs, the window open a crack and whistling. She thinks of what she did not say: eating cigarette butts in the girls' room, Brent's tongue in her mouth, his fingers prying at her crevices, Shelley carving "Donny" into her right arm, the men who followed her mother home. She thinks of her mother, rolling in now from a night serving beer, how she will look for her. He says nothing as he pulls into a Husky stop where she orders hot chocolate and a donut, watching him pour cream into his coffee with his calloused black hands, half expecting him to launch into rhyming tales of the north, like the ones she's been forced to memorize at school. But he is hunched over his cup now, under the weight of nothing ever turning out the way he dreams, of her mother's refusal to do as he says, of the endless road unrolling before him. And although she knows she is too old for dolls, it occurs to her that hers will not sleep tonight, that they will be stiff and lifeless in her pink room, waiting for her to do her rounds.

MOTEL SUMMER

In the motel there are a dozen units and several pads upon which small trailers sit. There is a woman with wild red hair who plays Janis Joplin so loud all of them know the words to "Me and Bobby McGee." Her mother says Janis has the voice of a wounded angel. She cries whenever a slow song winds its way into the room. There are kids everywhere. They play kick the can and every time she finds a good spot she loses because she can't leave. Once, she dug herself into a haystack with only a small hole to breath from and it wasn't until the sky was so black that the mountain behind the motel shifted and lost itself to the night that she could push out and run for the can. The motel is full of road builders. One of them takes her walking on hot afternoons and afterward her stomach aches. Her mother says she is not too old to nap and she lies on her double bed listening to the can slide across the pavement. Sometimes her mother lies with her back to her, singing along with Janis, waiting for her man to find his way home, for the maids to come, for lunch and a burger at the café down the street, for the hours to pass until the next bingo game, for this road to end, and the potential for magic with the next one.

LEARNING TO WINK

Life is hard her mother tells her. You have to go out of your way to make people smile because everyone wants to smile even though they get caught up in their lives, the details of which are sad and unimportant and can be released with a wink and a smile. Especially men, she says, who shoulder most of the worldly burdens. When she drives to the pharmacy, or for a cheeseburger at the Ho In, her mother makes a point of making men smile. At red lights she leans toward the window smiling at men in semis, or cabs. And soon, they are both winking at mailmen and city workers, ditchdiggers and traffic cops, she and her mother, sailing down city streets, highways and alleys, smiling, winking, nodding. Even in restaurants her mother goes out of her way to wink like that, and often the men pull a chair up to their booth, or offer to pay for their lunch, which is not the point, her mother says, politely refusing anything other than a good story in return. But sometimes they are insistent, following them through their day until they are forced to sneak out the back door of a restaurant, speeding away in the Chrysler, her mother laughing, hysterical, patting her on the knee, warning her to cross her legs, and hold on.

WALKING ON FIRE

The air is purple and smoky from piles of burning leaves. At the north end of the field a farmer stands by his tractor waving at her as she runs, and she's heard of trespassing and salt guns, which makes her run faster, tripping on the uneven earth below, hard chunks stubborn with woody stalks chopped by the steel of his plough. Where the pee has soaked into the denim, her thighs sting, and she knows that if she runs as fast as she can she might lift up and soar above the shifting mountains, away from the roads and schools, from the hands. She is running, the farmer is running, the red plaid of his shirt driving her further. And it is not until she is in the centre of the field that she feels the heat in her runners, that she stops to take a breath, smells the melting rubber, the embers alive and smoking underfoot.

BEAR HUNTING

Unlike her mother, who double-locked doors against them and threw a tantrum when her father got out of the car in a national park to feed one an ice cream cone, Tante Lolette sought them out. All that summer they searched for scratch marks, investigated turds. She shared her secret tree—a good place to spot bears if you could shimmy high enough—but Tante remained earthbound, clucking her tongue at her tales, saying *Oh-là-là* as she dove from the high rafters of the neighbour's barn, clapping as she rode their naggy mare bareback (without consent), marvelling at the anthill; so attentive as she instructed her on how to bang a nail, split shingles, call a chicken. In return Tante described the Alps, summer lantern processions in the valley, her classroom and lessons that made her envy the soft, elegant French girls she imagined sitting, like Madeline, in long, still rows. At night Tante undid the silver bun of her hair on one side of the bed, then walked around to the other side, the length of it unwinding. She brushed her hair: *les cheveux, la brosse, la nuit, l'ours*, she'd repeat as she stroked. On the last night of her visit they ate honey-dipped blackberries and she felt miserable for failing her. That night she dreamed of bears wearing tiaras, marching in rows under the Eiffel Tower, she and Tante on bicycles with lanterns humming "La Marseillaise." In the coolest part of the night she awoke to the sound of crashing metal. From her window she could see Tante's shawl, and before her a black bear rising on its hind legs, then the rifle's crack and zing. The bear's massive head swung from side to side with a roar that made her stomach vibrate, before it turned and crashed through the bush. *Mais, non*, she cried, *Non!* And even after the lights came on and the neighbour's dog started up, Tante lay, her ear to the ground, her hand in the massive print: *Mon dieux. C'est magnifique, hein? Magnifique.*

TEETHMARKS

Saturday morning and while her mother sleeps she sneaks over to Terry's house where there is a playroom and several dolls with various lengths of hair, as well as a Barbie house, Barbie car, and a pink overflowing Barbie carrying-case, which Terry opens and offers her a doll from. Terry dresses her own doll in formal eveningwear, styles her hair with tiny plastic combs. She undresses hers, stares at the plastic breasts, which have teeth marks on them. From the dog, Terry assures her, when he was a puppy. Terry pulls out a Ken doll, smooth and smiling, places it naked in her hand, her thumb resting on the form-fitted boxers. There is no taking them off. You could marry them, Terry decides, rummaging for a bridesmaid's dress. But before she knows it Ken pushes Barbie down on the floor and is humping her. Terry screams at her to stop, says it isn't funny but Ken goes on humping, and soon he is humping her right across the green shag carpet. Terry is crying now, her hands a furious windmill. She stands and steps right on her Barbie house. She grabs Ken and throws him across the room. She tells her to leave, shoving the clothes back into her wardrobe, the naked Barbie still smiling, Ken with his bum in the air.

THE LATIN MYSTERY

Her father is in town after a season of injuries and no work, no money, still, she knows there are ice skates under the tree they cut down from the riverbank. All night it has snowed, soft, forgiving flakes. He cracks walnuts, and her mother smokes. At midnight he puts on his boots and she follows him, cigar hanging from his mouth, hands clasped behind his back. They sit on the hard pews at the back of the church, her father taking deep breaths and longing for Latin, which is getting harder and harder to find he says, because of missals and bulls, the modernization of the church, a point he disagrees with in a sad, resigned way, because especially in this wild land of pioneering men, His lambs are lost. So lost that some days, he tells her, he is convinced he will never find the peace of God. And later, as they walk home, feet scrunching, snow falling so slow it seems to scarf around their ears, her cheeks hurt from the idea of him. And when she begins to skip ahead it is because she is laughing, because she believes these snowflakes will never melt.

Bridging & Tunelling

SURFACE

Mid-August, overheated, moorings cut, lives boxed,
we slog to the Danforth for souvlaki and iced lattes,
quick shots of the Barents Sea, 118 sailors suspended
in five hundred feet of steel, flickering on screens
in store windows, and tiny, over the cash register.
You say you don't want to leave, but who
can afford the luxury of home these days?
All that last night as you slept, I lay my cheek
on the cool floor of the echoing kitchen, listening
to overseas broadcasts and constant updates: the *Kursk*,
the longshots, the possibilities. I imagine Dmitri
and Alexei in their bunks, the notes, the last seconds.
Were they aware we were all listening? How we are all
in our wired worlds, on the bottom of the Barents,
tapping our goodbyes to the baleen whales.

THE DEATH OF THE MOTH

At first they were charming, the size of their powdery wings, the diamond back, common as house sparrows. They went at the bulb, one, and then two: tenacious wrong-headed boxers, and I marvelled at the simplicity of their nocturnal flight. But slowly, the irritation set in: the late-night headbanging, the wide swings and pillow plunges, the sudden scurry across the sheet, the quick flight from a book left on the sofa, a hat lifted from a chair. Sleepless, desperate, I began to catch them—first one, then two at a time—in an empty film canister. I let them go in the yard where they melted into the bark of a hemlock, feeling virtuous, a real mensch when it came to Nature; a real patron of the moth. But they would not give up. They dug at the screens, rooted themselves in the doorsill, half a dozen flying erratic at my face whenever I moved. And then the trapping became more haphazard. One dropped in a glass of water. *Let it die*, I thought, but next morning when I picked up the glass, its legs kicked and when I dumped the water in the yard, it righted itself and marched indignant across the grass and I vowed no more death. But still they came. And the next night a shoe flew across the room, followed by a book, a pillow, a box of Kleenex and still they came, still they showed no sense of decorum in their fluttering. Why the headbanging? Why the sporadic flight, the desire to burrow under my hair? If not for all these behaviours, the moth would be lovely. If not for the sheer numbers; if not for its mothness, if not for my humanness, if not for a house with sashes and sills, if not for a desire to read before sleep, the necessity of a bedside lamp, if not, I thought—for a one-crop world attracting one-bug problems. If not for all that I would not have to resort to the vacuum, hose in air, sucking winging moths, followed by a straight shot of Raid, until the house is wingless, the bag discarded, sheets turned back, nightlight burning, all the dark flutterings of the night safely contained.

VOYAGEUR

It started early
thinking the river
a conveyor belt,
trees stepladders
clouds a possibility,
who says feet
are for walking, wings
only for flight?
She set off carrying
almonds and fragments
that have pierced
twenty-six centuries,
sailing with the same
eyes Leif Eriksson
navigated icebergs
with, Marie Antoinette's
sick sense of humour, love
of sharp blades,
and hands that tossed
rocks onto Hannibal
crossing the alps;

continues through
this canyon city
infested with its yellow
beetles and steel
worms wriggling
under two rivers;
is a rusty track,
pissed on
still dreaming
home.

PENTECOSTAL FIGURES

Three feet tall they crowd together
like smokers on a coffee break.
The hands, all of them, suppliant
—no surprise there. Brows float
across polychrome haloed foreheads,
a picket fence of limbs nailed
to another halo and toes, urgent
somehow, not to have a groin, but toes.
The figures, their carbon-copy features:
beard, plaits, gaze
up into floodlights. Except
that one with real hair, darker
than the slickest stain, pinched
cheek and eye. She has waited
her whole life to arrive in the city,
is waiting for the lights to go down,
wanting to try on a pair of those
stilettos, slip out for some pastrami
and a tour of Harlem. She's
getting out now. She'll roll,
if she has to.

HOUSES

She made them of playing cards, egg cartons,
Popsicle sticks and twigs. Furnished them
with matchstick chairs, tables of crinkled
cigarette foil, tiny cotton puff beds.
She imagined them in the spiked
shadows of stairways, the silty, coal interiors
of things. She dug them under rocks,
and stumps, tunnelled into razor wire
brambles. She saw them in cardboard
from ring to shoe to packing
and once, big as a refrigerator.
They were possible in abandoned pickups,
school buses, rail cars, dumpsters. They
took shape in stacks of tires or palettes, rusted,
industrial waste. She felt them
a series of shrinking opportunities, under tables
and chairs, laundry basins, cupboards and drawers. Or,
of off-cut gyproc, two-by-fours, harvest
or avocado swatches of shag, climbing
what trees remained, her finger
on the hinge of space.

FORTY FAST APPROACHING

All is Pema: red oak, Provençal gold.
Desire a Zeppelin.

Squirrels eat tulips. Your lips
tangy. Eyes on springs.

Spring is a puddle in 1969: mojos
spearmint or banana. Sludge of toes.

Alone, seasick, this hooked year
on the verge of either falling or flying.

All knees in a drain your Spidey
wrists webbing tree roots, boulders.

Fast, fast, the ice cream is melting,
the children have all gone home.

Pillow of books. April, you have
not had a fresh thought in months.

On the edge, under the rush
of words, something opaque.

At ease, what you dream of
tastes like toffee, is a slower melting.

TONIGHT THE SKY IS MY BEGGING BOWL

While I savour woodstove-scented sleep,
you move in a forest of brick and glass: sleepless.

Your eyes droop, dreaming the half-point of grades
and coffee at the end of the picket line. Sleepy.

I dress in fleece, stalk blackberries for birds,
canes flattened from a winter storm as we slept.

I embrace everything, even the slither of midnight,
but without you, time is too wide, I cannot sleep.

Clatter of dragon paw—the old year retreats, tail between
her legs. This thumping new one will not sleep.

We are simply where we are. Me, alone
in silk and fleece, you on a subway deprived of sleep.

Tonight the sky is my begging bowl: wing tip,
wood thrush I open palms, heart, enclave of sleep.

SPANGLED

Rare vision, a Jersey cyclist on Route 1, even rarer
this one an ant waving a flag the size of a billboard.
Today, all flags at half-mast, TVs blaring on fifty-
two channels: the minutiae of grief.

Slender, fractured state of diners and tomatoes,
turnpikes and toll booths, pharmaceuticals and refineries:
the big apple inverted, tunnelled together and bleeding,
the *New York Times* delivered free to our doorstep

this morning, mourning in every section. And though
I too remember the dazed faces, spray of bone, shredded
notes, the smell—even months after, burned cotton candy
acrid in my throat—I can't help but wonder if the ad rates

went up or down on this day, can't help but weep
for the bloodbath this grief will unleash. And don't
think I don't know about anguish: it's that I hope mine
is dispersed, is not a sharp, spangled weapon. Now

the mechanic warns I am becoming unmuffled,
and I wonder who else is reading my mind?

DEAR FERRON

Cats and Redwoods. California sounds idyllic, forging
the two extremes, my body knows well, the frustration.
Envy the yurt, time, land, warmth—but not the isolation.
Unbalanced as usual, my wrought-iron life, but gorging
on culture: yesterday five galleries in Chelsea. Goldin's
Heartbeat, and Björk singing a Greek Orthodox Mass
the best antidote for empire I've seen in weeks. Alas
the rain. Umbrellaless through Washington Square holding
an *I ❤NY* bag overhead, Marilyn's latest fluttering under
my coat. Dinner at Dojo's an unglamorous affair.
What you say about the sham(e) of war is true. Where
did all those marchers go? Crossing Burrard, you thunder
on Sunset Beach. We blinked: our nightmares sprang
to life. And now those songs and placards out again.

SIGNS

The balcony is wet. Moss cowers where the door slides
open, clicks into place. Aspens quake. On the blue
light of the field below, six denimed teenagers
pass a glue-filled bag from mouth to mouth, blue-
lipped. Bell-bottomed women plough strollers. Smell
of rain, droplets on your hand, your future quivers blue
as mercury. In two minutes your mother will burst
through the door and in her grief, in her blue
plunge, knock the lampshade off its base, smash
the dish-stacked sink. You're watching for signs: blue
blood spilt, tears from a traffic light, trees growing
through metal, something warmer than blue.

EROS, OR ERROR

The door blows open and Sappho steals in, sits
on the side of the bed where you are moaning,
alone, longing to be larger than yourself.

There is dust on your lines, she says,
dull wit cramps your damp bed. Crack
your spine: it's about desire, the triangulation of,

intensity of the other, not self, split in two. And
not just any other, be discerning. Condense yes,
but expand. And you're wishing she

were more butch than you. That
she would expand you right now. But
already she is only shadow. Somewhere

the A-train stops and she stirs aboard. She
knows you ride it daily. Knows you will
follow. Knows it's a matter of time.

ACKNOWLEDGEMENTS

Thanks to Marilyn Hacker, Gabe Fried, Yerra Sugarman, Elaine Sexton, Martin Mitchell, Joy Katz, Todd Swift, Carol Moldaw, Arthur Sze, Diana Fitzgerald Bryden, Marlene Cookshaw, Margaret Webb, Mary di Michele, Ron Smith, Sally Cohen, Chris Banks, Don McKay and Danielle Bobker for valuable comments and support; thanks to Silas White and Triny Finlay for fine editing. Earlier versions of these poems appeared in *The Malahat Review*, *Grain*, *Descant*, *Rattapallax*, *7Carmine*, *nth position*, *Poets Against the War* and *Greenboathouse*. Thanks to the Dodge Foundation, The Vermont Center, Hedgebrook, Stegner House and the Banff Centre for the Arts.

Quote from John Berger, *Ways of Seeing*, used by permission of Penguin Group USA.